JONGLEUR

JONGLEUR

versions from the troubadours

RENNIE PARKER

All rights reserved. No part of this work covered by the copyright herein may be reproduced or used in any means – graphic, electronic, or mechanical, including copying, recording, taping, or information storage and retrieval systems – without written permission of the publisher.

Printed by imprintdigital
Upton Pyne, Exeter
www.digital.imprint.co.uk

Typesetting and cover design by The Book Typesetters
us@thebooktypesetters.com
07422 598 168
www.thebooktypesetters.com

Published by Shoestring Press
19 Devonshire Avenue, Beeston, Nottingham, NG9 1BS
(0115) 925 1827
www.shoestringpress.co.uk

First published 2021
© Copyright: Rennie Parker

The moral right of the author has been asserted.

ISBN 978-1-912524-93-8

ACKNOWLEDGEMENT

Several versions have appeared in *The High Window*, ed. David Cooke, February 2021.

for Bernard Parker
(1925–2020)

CONTENTS

Introduction	1
Bertran de Born (c.1140–1215)	
It pleases me, the merry springtime	5
Azalais de Porcairagues (d.1177)	
Now when the cold weather arrives	7
Marcabru (fl.1130–1148)	
At the beginning of winter	9
At the fountain in a garden	11
Peire Cardenal (1180–1278)	
I see the times have changed	13
On Esteve de Belmont, who annoys me	14
Rigaut de Berbezilh (c.1120–1180)	
Just as the elephant	16
Just as the lion	18
Na Castelloza (fl.1200)	
You have been so long at my house	20
I shouldn't have any desire to sing	22
Bernart de Ventadorn (c.1130–c.1190)	
You ask me sir	24
Giraut de Bornelh (1138–1215)	
This year I have no joy or consolation	26
Glorious king, true light and clarity	28
Peirol (1160–1272)	
When Love found I had left	30

Beatriz, Comtessa de Dia (fl.1178–1215)
    I am singing about what I don't want   32
    Fine joy grants me lightness   34

Guilhem de Peitieu (1071–1127)
    I will make a verse about nothing   35

Arnaut Daniel (1150–1210)
    The bitter wind   37
    Songs are made with fine clear words   40

Gaucelm Faidit (fl.1172–1203)
    From the vast depths of the sea   42

Garsenda de Forcalquier (1180–1242)
    You seem to have the heart of a lover   44

Jofre Rudel (fl.1120–1147)
    When the days are long in May   45

Notes   47
Further Reading   51

INTRODUCTION

There are more than enough trobar (troubadour) poems describing the springtime and how a poet's thoughts turn to love. And there are plenty of verses in the repertoire where the poet is discussing 'proesa' (prowess) or the 'pretz' (worth, worthiness) of a lover or lord. In providing a new selection, I set out with the intention of finding works which brought some context about the period (c.1050–1300), showing something of the expectations placed on poets at the time, or hints from their shared heritage and how it reaches forward to inform poets in later centuries. As well as poets listening to birdsong in the woods, we have the Comtessa de Dia complaining about her man, Guilhem de Peitieu satirising the poetic genre he helped to create, and Peire Cardenal's reactions on finding that his current appointment is worse than his previous one. Despite the remoteness of 12th century Occitania, emotions and dilemmas result in poems we can recognise, even though the place is otherwise distant and mysterious, populated with self-contained fiefdoms in what became the southern half of France.

Very little is known about the poets other than what they reveal in their works. Some were from the provincial nobility, while others held positions in a lord's household, or fulfilled duties in the clergy or the military. Others were trained musicians or singers with the equivalent of a contract to provide entertainment at a specific court; and a player might migrate from one to another during the course of his or her career. A poet might be a writer-performer, or working in association with a colleague who performed the songs on his behalf. The name of this interpreter (the 'juglar' or 'jongleur') is sometimes recorded along with the creator. Song and poem appear as more or less interchangeable, and some form of musical accompaniment was expected.

Unlike elsewhere in feudal Europe, it was possible for a low-status individual to achieve fame and fortune in Occitania through their writing skills: Marcabru and Giraut de Bornelh followed this pattern. Women fared much better than in other countries, with some rights to individual wealth and property.

Education was possible, which – together with a room of her own – enabled the trobairitz to achieve recognition as a creator in her own right. Much critical work has been done since the 1980's to elevate the female repertoire, and it is safe to say that while only a fraction of the work survives, anonymous poems are just as likely to be the work of a trobairitz as a trobar. The poets frequently practised debates in verse ('tenso') and it was usual for a male/female pairing to work on a long poem.

We cannot read far into medieval verse without coming across courtly love, or 'fin amor' as it was usually termed. This structured behaviour was a convenient way of handling alternative relationships in a period when people could be married off for reasons of inheritance and power. Sometimes a player in the game of fin amor would achieve his or her objective; more often, pursuit and evasion were the whole point of the exercise, resulting in songs and verses being exchanged and love triangles ennobled through an atmosphere of chivalry and honour. There was (in addition) a distinction between fin amor at the castle and carnal love as experienced by the population at large, which did not have the same layers of symbolism and gamesmanship. Peasant mistresses and comedy husbands are generally treated with irony and earthy humour, similar to Chaucer's depictions in *The Canterbury Tales*. It is unclear how seriously the poets bought into the idea of fin amor, since many of them performed their work as a career, dependent on patronage from the players of courtly love for their incomes.

In providing new versions of the poems included here, I have attempted to stay as close as possible to the original lines, although this meant sacrificing the rhyme schemes in each case. Happily, some poems developed enough assonance and incidental rhyme for a reader to gain an impression of the galloping rhythms and tight stanzas found in the original. Occitan has a higher frequency of rhyming words than English, and any attempt to copy the rhyme schemes would inevitably take the text further away from the poets' intentions. The blunt language and no-nonsense attitudes encountered in some of the poems are there in the original, creating an effect which is at odds with the popular image of a lovelorn minstrel.

In a couple of instances, missing and conjectural lines are indicated by [ ], while puzzling references are explained in the notes on pp. 47–50. Envoys – effectively the speaking poet's sign-off – are provided as indented blocks, as are any poems where more than one character appears in the same verse. I have also looked for poems where the tunes are still available, either as transcripts or recordings online. The Jofre Rudel 'lanquan li journ' and Bornelh's 'reis glorios' are often found in early music compilations, and their haunting melodies are still a source of inspiration for composers today.

> Rennie Parker, April 2021.

BERTRAN DE BORN
'Be.m platz lo gai temps de pascor'

It pleases me, the merry springtime
When foliage happens and the flowers appear
It pleases me also, the liveliness
Of the birds, who bring back
Their song to the woods;
And it pleases me when I see the meadows
Sealed over with heaven's pavilions
And I have great happiness
When I see how the companies gather,
Cavalry and armed horses.

And I am pleased when the vanguard
Sends the people into flight
And it pleases me when I see afterwards
Great armies coming together
And it pleases me and my courage
When I see strong castles under siege
Their ramparts wrecked and collapsing,
And I see the host on the banks
Where all around are trapped in the ditches
Enclosed by heavy timbered palisades.

And this is also a lord's pleasure,
When the first ones are attacking
On armed horses without fear
And how they increase in boldness
With honourable service
And then, how they engage in combat
Everyone must be ready
To follow with willingness
Because no man has any worthiness
When there is a fault in his approach.

Mattocks and swords, painted helmets
Shields cut down and destroyed,
We see them at the start of battle

And many vassals fighting together –
They give themselves to the cause,
Horses of the dead and of the injured,
And when he is engaged in battle
Every man of noble honour
Does not think anything of splitting heads and arms
Because he would rather be dead than vanquished.

And I have to admit I take no pleasure
Eating without butter and not sleeping
Except when everyone roars 'At them!'
On both sides and each boasts
Riderless horses in the shade,
Each person crying out 'Help! Help!'
And I see falling into the pits
Small and large onto the grass
And I see the dead with their sides run through
By lances with their pennants.

> Worthy comtessa, the greatest
> Whose example we follow, wonder of wonders,
> Your man is enthralled by the best-born
> Woman in the world, as everyone agrees,
> Beatritz of the high lineage
> Great lady in words and in deeds,
> Origin of song and source of all beauty
> Lovely in her majesty,
> Your high worth is elevated so much
> Who is exalted above all others.

> Baron, spending and forfeiting
> Castles and towns and cities,
> Advance when everyone is your enemy.
> Papiol, with willing obedience
> Go straight to 'Yes-and-No' and say to him
> We have been at peace too long.

AZALAIS DE PORCAIRAGUES
'Ar em al freg temps vengut'

Now when the cold weather arrives
With the ice and the snow and the mire
And the little birds are silent
When it's not warm enough to sing
And the leaves are dry in the hedges,
No rumour of flowers and foliage
No rumour of any nightingales,
When will love and Maytime return to me?

Now I have a broken heart
Because I'm estranged from everyone
And I know how a person is lost
Most of all when they're gaining nothing –
And I make these truthful words:
D'Aurenga is my destiny
For when I delay my delight in him
Ruin is all I am left with.

A woman unfortunate in love
Who would match with a worthy man
Should go much higher than a *vavassor*
Otherwise she makes a mistake.
I say: as a man grows older
His grandeur is not so real
And women who have no discernment
Will lower themselves in value.

I have a friend of great renown
Who is above all other lords
And his heart does not deceive him
About me, whose love is guaranteed.
I say that our love is destined
And those who say it's not so
God send them ill fortune
While I remain strong and secure.

Sweet friend with a fine disposition
Every day is a good one with you,
Courtesy and a handsome appearance,
Your demands are never outrageous
Or we'll soon be tested and tried
If your mercy's not granted to me;
You may give me a caution
But you'll never say it's my fault.

To God I commend Belesgar
The best in the town of Aurenga
And Gloriet and the castle
And the *seigneur* of Provence.
I wish them all the best there
At the arch with the battle upon it
I would give my life to him
And I am distressed forever!

> Player with a happy heart
> Carrying this song to Narbonne
> My song is at an end:
> May Joy and Youth be your guide.

MARCABRU
'Al prim comens de l'invernaill'

At the beginning of winter
When acorns rain in the woods
I wish men would engage themselves
On security; those who do not weave
And those who are not in love
As if they were still in the green time.

Well, every other fellow complains
When he sees cold weather and mud
Ganging up against him –
Why isn't he ready and bartering
When in summer you don't need clothes,
When you can walk in bare skin?

These ones are just like animals
Full and glutted in the evening
After the wine –
Never giving a thought to tomorrow
And these grey losers swear
They have never seen such bad times.

Young men of handsome appearance
I see them ruined by villainy,
Who go around boasting –
They say, devising a thousand projects
'We will make them when the weather is fine'
Yet everything remains as bluster and noise.

And they have the habits of children
Who say: when there is light
He will build a house –
But when it is there and you tell him
He neither listens nor hears
And for him there is nothing to do.

Husbands! The best in the world
You are… but chastise your mistress,
Why are you confounded
When she puts herself on the market
Because of a young vagabond
And you are called a cuckold?

The price is shame and fraud
Wherever it comes from
Even the husband –
And I have the answers for you,
Where happiness is spread between you
And money maintains you all.

The wrongs and the rights are above us
And youth will declare its losses
From the lowest to the highest.
Sadly, I find what is freely given –
Hats will fly at a vile accuser,
A scapegoat, without any knowledge.

MARCABRU
'A la fontana del vergier'

At the fountain in a garden
On the grass just near an orchard
In the shade of a fruit tree branch
Where the white flowers arranged
Themselves like a new song
I found her alone, without friends
She who does not love me.

This girl with her lovely shape
Daughter of a castle lord
And when I thought how the birds
Were making joy in the greenery
Concluding their new song sweetly
And who would listen to my noise,
Suddenly I found her changed.

Her eyes poured tears by the fountain
And sighs came from her heart:
'Jesu,' said she, 'King of the world
To you I cry out my sorrow
Now you have confirmed it
When the best in all the world
Goes to serve and to honour only you.

He has gone with you; my friend
Loveliest of men, so strong and proud
I am left with distress in exchange
My desire lies only in weeping
Alas, I curse King Louis
Who took those hands to his service –
Now sorrow destroys my heart,'

When I heard her so unhappy
I came close to the clear river.
'Pretty one,' I said to her, 'So much crying
Will spoil the colour in your complexion –

Don't you be so despairing
When He who bids this flourishing tree
Can give you the comfort of consolation,'

'Sir,' said she, 'I can well believe
That God will help me with mercy
In the other world, with bliss
When I rest there with other sinners
But I know this king has taken away
Every joy I had, and left me with nothing,
He who was so faithful to me.'

PEIRE CARDENAL
'Lo segle vei chamjar'

I see the times have changed
Because – my verses and songs –
I don't know where they have gone,
When one who is used to giving
Sees suffering all around him
And questions the whole of life.
And I who was used to my lover
In my arms both night and day
To hold and to kiss,
I cannot do anything about it –
Look, this is my life.

My life, it seems to me
I cannot possibly endure it
Under such conditions as these
For I would normally travel by horse
And refuse to wear clothing like this,
And peace will never happen
Because I don't know you any more,
Joys nor songs nor lover;
I have become so discouraged,
[My reputation fading]
Through bad government.

PEIRE CARDENAL
'D'Esteve de Belmon m'enueia'

On Esteve de Belmont, who annoys me
Because he is so fat and wobbly
And he pays his servants badly
And he jousts with the son of a sow.
And the leaders of the church are mistaken
That the fiercest traitor is nowhere –
There is no bad thing nor dishonour
In which Esteve is not a factor.
Hosts and pigs and servants
Everyone will be afraid of him
Whoever can be afraid;
These ones he kills with great pleasure.

Esteve, I will slide a remark
Into an ointment with some oil.
There are traitors who have no shame,
But the strongest traitors don't need any;
This hated man should be banished
From the sea as far as Burgundy.
[   ]
You have chosen your skinful of violence
A skinful of prayer most deceitful –
You are the man they make liquor of
They will use to anoint other traitors.

Esteve is careful, this heavyweight who watches
When in the chancel – a place seized –
He loves to fish for sinners
Traitoresses estranged from God
In nothing are they not betrayed.
Now look how the people become broken
And in pieces on this earth,
Stealing their compensation –
But a sinner has the greatest sorrow
When they sin with this pig of the pasture
Then they are named a sinner.

Esteve with the great big head
And the round belly like a roof-boss
His shoulders resemble burdens
I see nowhere in the world such uneven bones.
And you lie down with an aged red face
With lines thrown across it –
Esteve, I won't be concerned
When you are hung, when you are howling
And your faults are howling too,
When you are being eaten by vultures
They will leave your face alone.

Esteve, who doesn't know Justice
Wages serious war against thieving,
Who cannot bark any reprimand
[   ]
By God, I believe that when you're hung
You will swindle all the other felons
Of their ropes, fetters and tortures,
Who of clergymen carries no honour
Neither in clergying nor in sanctity:
Who, when you are serving Our Lord
Esteve, you would swindle even then.

> Eating killed his predecessor
> And a child of his lordship –
> By this he is named a traitor.

RIGAUT DE BERBEZILH
'Atressi con l'orifanz'

Just as the elephant
Who, when it falls, cannot rise up
By crying out toward the others with its voice
Since the others are raised above it with their noise
I will follow this example:
Since my troubles are heavy burdens
At the court of Puy with its extravagance
And the true worth of a loyal lover
No longer stands up, it will never be revealed
Who drives himself mad with asking for mercy –
There, one's prayers and mercy have no value.

And I am here as the lover
Who cannot return to happiness
By always singing my songs –
They no longer mean anything to me
So I will become like a hermit
Alone, by myself, such is my disposition
And my life annoys me with its pains
And joys are my dole and pleasures are my sorrows
Since I cannot act in the manner of a bear
Who, when the villains bait him without mercy
Grows larger with increasing rage.

It's good to know that Love has so much greatness
That I could be pardoned –
It is my fault I have loved too much,
I did not fly high like Dedalus
Who said when he was at leisure
He would throw himself into the sky with outrageous vanity
But God brought down his pride and arrogance.
My pride is in nothing except my loving
For this I will be helped by Mercy
When now I have a reason for mercy to come
For in this place rights and reasons have no value.

The whole world and its clamour
Around me, and too much talking –
If I could imitate you,
Phoenix, a gift not otherwise given –
When you burn you can resurrect above,
But I will be burnt by so much embarrassment:
My fault the words in my messages are mistaken.
I will resurrect in sighs and in tears
There in beauty and youth and valour;
It is not my fault that a small amount of pity
Will not reveal to anyone who means well.

My songs and their effects,
Verses which no-one is going to hear
And regard with true insight –
So many of them locked up and imprisoned
And I am the man with no excuses
Greatest of women, I have been gone for two years.
Look around at the sorrow and tears for you,
Just as the deer, who, when it has run its course
Turns and is killed at the cries of its hunters
So I turn, Lady, to you for your mercy
But you do not care, since you do not believe in love.

>Just as the lord who brings many blessings
>Every day when I see you I cannot find fault.
>Dear Bericle, joy and honour to you;
>I have all I want when you remember me.

RIGAUT DE BERBEZILH
'Atressi com lo leos'

Just as the lion
Who is so fierce when angry
Over his lioncub when it is born
Dead without breath and without life
And with his voice, when he roars
To make it revive and move –
In this way, on my behalf
My good Lady and Love
Will fight against my sorrows.

All the joyful seasons
Arrive in April and May;
Good fortune will come to me
From now on –
Love has been asleep too long
For those who can give to Love
Their ardent prayers.
Ah, so much great honour –
I am all hesitation and fears.

Rich will be the reward
Peaceful words, honest words
My pleasure to have them,
If her pity does not forget me
Like a lost ship
Where none can escape
Without strong swimming –
In this way, Lady, I will revive
With a little assistance.

Worried by needs and joys,
Often I sing, often I'm angry
Sometimes thinner, sometimes fatter,
In this way I am divided

By Love's delights and troubles.
It's with laughing and with playing
With cares and with thoughts
Showing their deeper meanings
To me between the laughter and tears.

All the best features
Of the world are in you; and besides
Lady, there is nothing you lack –
You are filled with all virtues.
If you would be an ardent lover
Nothing else improves one so much;
In all these you are without equal
And the walls and castles and towers
Of Honour and Beauty flourish.

Lady, God save you and guard you
No man could be greater
In praise of you –
For you I am slain by Love
My soul and my heart have departed
I am no longer here in my body,
I know of no other bounty
I would reach for, neither walls nor towers.

NA CASTELLOZA
'Mout avetz fach long estatge'

You have been so long at my house
My friend, and now you have left me:
I am doleful and dissatisfied
Because you swore to me and declared
That all the days of your life
You would have no other woman but me.
If you take another
You will leave me dead and betrayed,
I have my hopes in you
Who loves me, without a doubt.

Dear friend, with my fine heart
I loved you; we were successful
And I know how foolish I have been –
(I am very much destined towards it)
I was never dishonest with you
But you've done bad instead of good
Though I love you without regret,
Since love has seized me so hard
I do not believe in its bounty
Unless I can have your loving.

I have heard about the awful habits
Of those other lovers
Who send their messages to men
In words selected and arranged
And I am ready for opposition –
My friend, by my faith
When you plead, anyone would agree
That the highest would not be annoyed
If they had an abundance from you
Of kisses or charming behaviour.

I get no good from you and your fickle heart
You have been too changeable,
And a lover with no honour

Cannot be an embarrassment for me.
Yet I am pensive and troubled
Because my love is not as I dreamed
And I have no enjoyment from you.
Soon you will find me finished
By only a small amount of illness –
I'm a dead woman if a man does not cure me.

All the mistreatment and the shame
Which is my fate with you….and yet
You have pleased my parents
And above all my husband.
If you have done any wrong towards me
I pardon it, in good faith
And pray that you will return to me
In spite of hearing what you hear,
My song, which is made in truth:
You will find it a perfect likeness.

NA CASTELLOZA
'Ia de chantar non degra aver talan'

I shouldn't have any desire to sing
Because whenever I sing
It's worse for me in love
When complaints and tears
Make their home in me,
Which is a great pity
To have between my heart and me.
And soon I won't restrain myself –
I have waited in vain too long.

Despite having been at your command
And then some,
My friend, I've not had much
For all my pleading –
You do not send me any letters
How can I have free rein?
My friend, you have done nothing.
Now joys do not sustain me:
A little sorrow is not enough.

Let me help you remember in song
How I had your glove
Which I stole, trembling –
Then I was afraid
It would bring shame upon you
If that item was kept by me.
My friend, straightaway
I returned it to you, knowing all too well
I did not have your permission.

Some knights I know who will shame themselves
Because they are pleading
Many women who are theirs –
This is another level,
With no shame or hierarchy in it.
When women are in love

They must plead well for a knight
When they see in them
Great prowess and chivalry.

BERNART DE VENTADORN
'Pois preyatz me, senhor'

You ask me sir
If I sing, if I will sing.
My song's cut short, I cry
The minute I begin.
It's miserable for your singer
Who sings when all's not well –
What can be done when love's gone wrong
And the best one can't be had?
Now, why am I so mad?

It's an honour great and good
To know God's on my side
When I love the best of all
And she loves me, I know.
But it will never be, alas
I don't know how she fares –
I'm killing myself with sorrow,
I don't have the occasion,
I dream of going there.

It increases so my wound
Because she is my dream
That's why I cry my lament
But nobody hears a thing.
So sweetly she deceives
The heart right out of me
That I can't say who I am
And imagine or believe
What my eyes may never see.

Love, what will I do?
Shall we battle, me and you
To be ended when I'm dead
Of longing when I see
The loveliest where she is?

I hear nothing close to her
With her caresses and blonde hair
Undressing in my sight
White body round and light.

I'm not discouraged by loving
By misfortune, neither pain
Since God will keep me well –
I'll soon bounce back from scorn
And I'm not unprepared;
I can well put up with shame
As my prayers will allow
When a man is pushed back down
The more he leaps around.

Good lady, please have mercy
On your fine high-minded love!
Hands together, with neck inclined
I'm waiting on your command
Who pleads here in good faith
Who loves no other so much
That sometimes I'm improved
You make me look more handsome
Whose most is not so grand.

> My Escudar and me
> Give hearts and minds to God
> That we may never stray
> As long as He's with us
> From where our talent comes
> And he is My Love.

GIRAUT DE BORNELH
'S'anc journ agui jai ni solatz'

This year I have no joy or consolation,
I am angry
And always in despair
Since I cannot change my future
Or recover happiness
Because I am pierced
By what remains in my thoughts
While I lament my lost friend.

Like my cries were expressed when I was born
As if God was not pleased,
Why does my brave best friend
Not live any more when other people do?
Thus it is my destiny
I do not have my Linhaure, which troubles me,
My greatest joy has fallen first
And thus begins my misery.

Now everyone will recognise me
As a man forsaken
Because of you, Linhaure, my loved one
Now I will be so downhearted
Since I will no longer see you,
Never to arrive at where you are
With your welcome and courteous messages,
Giver of joy who became everything to me.

To a fine friend and his *savoir-faire*
Foolhardy in deeds,
And honour and cleverness with his memory:
For you were struck down during April and May
The bittersweet season
And I will never be cheerful again
And I will never sing spontaneously,
Now it can only be a mournful summer.

You contained so many qualities
That you were lacking in nothing –
I was never your equal in poetry.
Now I cannot come and see you again
So much will not exist
Of the only man with such prowess;
There was no knight with the gift of words
Who won so many laurels.

Dead are his beautiful follies
And joy in words,
And deeds and women forgotten –
(Any 'ruined reputation' was restored by you….)
Through the gate at Velay
Now I will become wretched,
Whom you made guide and companion
Learning more about the mystery.

All your refined poems
About the good times
Of their worth, the judgement and the richness
And your desire for happiness,
All these become fouled –
I will not abandon anything of yours
When the brave lord of the Berengers
Is re-assembled by slanderers.

They say that by your legacy
Proensa is made magnificent
Nowhere else has so many works.
My Above-All, I have been killed;
The heart in me must write this letter.

GIRAUT DE BORNELH
'Reis glorios, verais lums e clartatz'

Glorious king, true light and clarity,
Most powerful god, Lord, if it pleases you
Lend your faithful aid to my companion
Whom I have not seen since I left him this night,
   and soon it will be dawn.

Good friend, whether you are sleeping or waking
Do not sleep too much; rise yourself up
For in the east I see the morning star
That heralds the day, I know it well
   and soon it will be dawn.

Good friend, I appeal to you in song:
Do not sleep too much, for I hear the birds singing
Who go searching for daylight in the woods
And I am afraid the jealous one will assail you
   and soon it will be dawn.

Good friend, come over to the window
And look at the stars in the sky!
Do you not know their faithful message,
'Where nothing is done, the shame is not on you'
   and soon it will be dawn.

Good friend, ever since I parted from you
I have neither slept nor got off my knees
But I prayed to God, the son of St. Mary
That I might remain your loyal companion,
   and soon it will be dawn.

Good friend, out there on the pavement
You begged me not to let you sleep; above all
To watch all night through until day –
You are no longer pleased with my song and my presence
   and soon it will be dawn.

Good sweet friend, I am in such a fine place
I don't want to know if it is dawn or day
Because the most beautiful one ever born from a woman
I hold in my arms, and therefore I fear
                neither the jealous fool nor the dawn.

PEIROL
'Quant Amors trobet partit'

When Love found I had left
My heart to its thoughts
On a song which displeased me
And could he hear my call:
>Friend Peirols, shame on you!
>You've been away so long
>And then, not a song –
>I don't know your intentions.
>Tell me, how can I help you?

Love, I have served you so much
I sought for nothing, took nothing
And you know how little
I've had of happiness –
I've had no opportunity.
The only thing you can do from now on:
Grant peace, that's all I ask for
Since no other benefits
Can ever be so powerful.

>Peirols, you must forget them
>The good and honourable lady
>Who welcomes you above all
>And so many people in love,
>All under my command –
>Your manner is far too light
>And it was only a dream
>Too much playing and too many lovers
>Were in your songs.

Love, it was not my fault –
Look how I am deserted
And praying to Lord Jesus my guide
And sending messages to Him
About reconciling the kings
Since help will arrive too late

And they are in great need,
Where the nobles, brave and strong
Otherwise have no companions.

>Peirols, Turks and Arabians
>Won't leave the Tower of David
>Because of your invasion.
>Great advice you're giving to your people
>Only about loving and singing!
>Get angry; and the king who isn't there
>When you see the wars they make –
>And yet they look after the barons
>Whenever they find it convenient.

Love, if the king doesn't go
You can say the same of the dauphin.
This war is not for you,
Don't worry about the valour.

>Peirols, many friends are leaving
>Their sorrowing lovers –
>Then, if the Saladins do nothing
>You can look upon their joy.

BEATRIZ, COMTESSA DE DIA
'A chantar m'er de so q'ieu non volria'

I am singing about what I don't want,
I am so angry at the one I love
Because I love no-one else except him
But he does not value my mercy nor my courtesy
Nor my beauty nor my position nor my good sense –
In this way he has betrayed and deceived me
As he would do if I was hideous to him.

It brings me comfort that I had no doubt
My love, that I was never arrogant towards you
I loved you not like Segui did Valensa
And it pleases me much how I won your love
Dear friend of mine, because you are so worthy;
Now you are proud to me in speech and behaviour
And yet you are open with everyone else.

I am amazed at how your body has become so proud
My friend, to me, and it gives me cause for complaint –
Nothing is right now this other love takes you away from me
For no-one else has the words and the welcome
And may I remind you of the beginning
Of our love? Mother of God I would never wish
It was my fault that you have left me.

The great prowess which lives in you
And the rich worthiness you have, it has disturbed me
I do not know any woman, near or far
If she wants to love, who would not be inclined towards you
But you, my friend, you realise only too well
What it is to have known the best one;
And may I remind you of what we have shared together.

As good as reducing my worth and my nobility
And my beauty and most of all my fine courage;
Therefore I send this verse to your estate
This song, which is my messenger

And I want to know, the best of all my friends,
Why are you being so fierce and vulgar towards me?
I don't know if it is pride or bad disposition.

But above all I want you to say, messenger
That too much pride is no good for any man.

BEATRIZ, COMTESSA DE DIA
'fin joi me don alegranssa'

Fine joy grants me lightness
And so I sing more gaily
I don't waste time on pensiveness
There's never a gloomy thought.
I know there's ones who'd shame me
False tale-telling sneaks and liars
Well, their bad words won't hurt me –
And so I'm twice as happy.

I'll never give my loyalty
To gossip-spreading tricksters
One cannot have integrity
Agreeing with such friends –
They are showing other faces
And their clouds fill up the spaces
Till the sun has lost its shine – I've
No love for folk like them.
And you, the jealous slanderer
Who thinks I won't be staying
Or that joy and youth don't please me:
Such lies will be your downfall.

GUILHEM DE PEITIEU
'Farai un vers de driet nien'

I will make a verse about nothing
Not about me or anyone else
Not about love or youth
Or anything at all. Rather
I'll make it while I am sleeping
On my horse.

I don't know what time I was born
Whether I am lively or annoyed
I am neither a stranger nor local,
Nothing I can do about it –
I'm worried I was enchanted by fairies
Languishing under a hill somewhere.

I don't know whether I'm sleeping
Or if I'm awake, if nobody tells me –
My heart isn't broken into small pieces
By a great sorrow,
And I'm worth no more than a cheese,
By St. Martial.

Unfortunately, I believe I will die –
I don't know when I will hear of it
I will ask the Doctor's opinion on me
But I don't know what he means.
Brave Doctors can defend me –
But no, not if they're bad ones.

I have a girlfriend here but I don't know who she is
Neither can I see her, so help me,
I have neither pleasure nor peace
But I don't care
Since neither a Norman nor a Frenchman
Have been in my house.

Since I don't see her and love the best
Since I have no rights and I have done no wrong,
When I don't see her, when it comes to making love
The game isn't worth it,
Whether I know she is the best and most beautiful
And whether she has value.

I have made the verse, don't know what it's about
And I'll send it to someone
Who will send it to someone else
Going towards Poitiers
Who will put it in his box
The prisoner.

ARNAUT DANIEL
'L'aura amara'

The bitter wind
Tears down foliage, emptying
Where sweet winds grew leaves
And the free beaks
Of the hedged birds
Stay silent and shut,
Partners and non-partners.
Why am I forcing myself
Into doing and saying mere trifles
At the hands of her
Who has me spinning from low to high
On pain of death,
Troubled when she does not adore me?

Now I will make clear
My first dawning
Of election –
She, with belief in her heart and eyes –
Unworthy, nothing,
Turned to bitterness
Those others; became
Rare, my pleadings –
Perhaps carried away
In my adoration, willingly –
Powerful secret words
For She who was such a magnet to me,
One who would serve her
Completely, at any asking.

Love, beware!
Am I welcome? Chosen,
Being humble, if unwelcome –
Such words, slights
Who gives me so many cuts
When I am made lover,
Dear, and never waver –

But the body is firmly closed
Which I would covet:
Many songs
From whom, with all the negatives
Would still have kisses at their choosing
Heart restored,
Who wants no other repairing.

If I am protected
From betrayal, from torment
If I have superior worth
In the quest, prayers
Which I hold inside me
Will keep me strong,
Clarifying my thoughts:
How I would be dead
But for the hopes
In these prayers I clamour,
Troubled when free, and yet bound –
For who can have enjoyment
When joy has no more value than an ornament?

Sweet face, with
Everything I wanted
Enduring through your pride
Which is odd
Through all my agitation
At the cruel hands
Of equals and backbiters
Who slander your name;
And I take my leave
Since they are not lovers –
Never so many who love ostentation
And also they desire you
Higher than God in the Cathedral.

It is like
Song and performance, created
For a king who welcomes it

When its value
Has decreased –
I know there it is doubled,
And maintenance, gifts and food
The happiness it brings,
His miraculous ring
Which he offers,
Who also would not be
One day in Aragon where it is dry
Where we do not wish to go,
When I know I can ask for Rome.

        I have made it
        For her heart's memory
        At her service
        She in courtesy,
        Her partner Arnaut
        Who would never imagine
        Any other would take his attention.

ARNAUT DANIEL
'Chansson do il mot son plan e prim'

Songs are made with fine clear words
I will do it when the buds are lively
And the highest tips
Are the colours
Of many flowers
And verdant the foliage –
And the songs and the notes
Are under the shades
With the birds and their tunes.

With the tunes I hear songs and refrains
By these I don't make them badly,
Worked and well-shaped
Tales of valour
With the art of Love –
I do not have the heart to turn from it
When it is faint
Dry and difficult:
One may regard me with pride.

There is little honour in lovers' pride
Thrown far from his lordship
On its high place –
Under the earth
For so much trouble,
Whose joys are diminished
Rights are less,
And it is pain and cuts
For those who argue against Love.

By arguing one sees nothing, alas –
Good lady whom I adore
But out of fear
From discovering
Where happiness is hidden

And appears as what they are not,
And we have no enjoyment
From its nourishment –
Bad is their outcome.

I will go where all is sorrowful –
My thoughts on song assail you
I who would sing
Of joys without end,
Songs on parting,
So many memories misting my eyes
From the anger and tears
And the sweetness,
Because I have joy with my pains.

I have love-hunger, who gapes on
And none of my measures are right,
Usually so equal,
And none of them heard
Since the time of Cain –
A lover without welcome,
Treacherous heart
And deceitful –
From this my happiness is raised.

      Lovely one, who would turn away…
      Arnaut's honest heart
      Sings in your honour
      Because your worth is placed above all.

GAUCELM FAIDIT
'Del gran golfe del mar'

From the vast depths of the sea
And the boredom of the journey
And of all perilous things
I have escaped, thank God!
Now I can speak and explain
How many miseries
I have suffered, and how much torment!
And please God, may I return
To Limousin, with a rejoicing heart
I left there in heaviness
I return there celebrating,
Delighted to show my gratitude.

The good God in his mercy
Willed that I, sane and strong
Could return to my country –
One has more there with a small garden
Than to live in other places –
Rich with great happiness
With the best welcome
And festivities and kind words,
My lady with her gifts
And loving behaviour,
Her sweet face
Seen in no other land.

I have the right to song
I can see joy and release,
Solace and chivalry
Where you are at peace;
And the fountains and clear streams
Make me lighthearted,
Fields and gardens and all my people.

I will have no more fear of sea and wind
West, Mistral, or East

And unsteady ships
And no more worries about
Galleys and racing corsairs.

Whoever would be saved by God
Take this discouragement from me
And save your soul
Good and right, nothing wrong.
But look here, if you would steal
And come to a bad end
Go to sea, where you will have a terrible time –
After a while it usually happens
That when you rise up you descend
And with total despair
You leave everything and throw it –
The soul and the body, the gold and the silver.

GARSENDA DE FORCALQUIER
'Vos que.m semblatz dels corals amadors'

You seem to have the heart of a lover
But I wish you were not so hesitant.
It pleases me greatly when we embrace in love
Otherwise I would be embarrassed for you,
Having so much shame in your cowardice
Because no one dares to ask for more boldness –
It would bring great shame on both of us
Since no woman dares to reveal
Above all that she wants these fears and misgivings.

JOFRE RUDEL
'Lancan li journ son lonc e may'

When the days are long in May
I hear sweet birdsong from afar
And when I have left that place
I remember a faraway love.
Then I go frowning and downcast
So that neither song nor hawthorn flowers
Please me any more than winter's ice.

I hold in truth to the Lord
Who has created this faraway love
But for every good thing in my destiny
I have double dole because I am far away.
Ah, why didn't I go there as a pilgrim
So that my rough clothing and hooded cloak
Would be recognised by her lovely eyes.

It will be joyful when I ask of her
For the love of God, a lodging over there
And, if it pleases her, I will stay
Close to her, although I am far away,
Where also we may talk together –
When distant lovers are seen so close
With courtesy they bring solace and pleasure.

Angry and sorrowful I will depart
If I do not see this faraway love.
I do not know when I will see her
Because our lands are so far apart
Countered by passes and roads
And such things must not separate me –
But all may be how she pleases.

Nevermore will I enjoy love
If I cannot enjoy this faraway love,
I do not know a greater or more beautiful one
In any place near or far

Whose qualities are so rich and consoling
That there in the Saracen's realm
I would declare myself a prisoner for her.

God who makes all that comes and goes
And created this faraway love
Give me the strength when I do not have the heart
So I might see this faraway love:
Truly in that distant place
How the rooms and gardens
Seem like new palaces to me.

He says the truth who calls me greedy
In longing for the faraway love,
Because no other joys please me so well
Except the enjoyment of the faraway love:
But what I want is forbidden to me, alas
And so it seems I am fated
That I love and I may not be loved.

NOTES

Bertran de Born's sword-rattling poem was famously translated by Ezra Pound. The frequency of wars and disputes meant that any lord had to be ready for battle, under a feudal obligation to the next rank in the heirarchy.

p.6, ll.31–33: Papiol is Bertran's jongleur and messenger; 'Yes-and-No' is Richard 1 of England (1157–1199), ruler of Aquitaine and Gascony at the time.

Azalais de Porcaraigues also worked as a musician. This is her only surviving poem.

p.7, l.19: vavassor – a middle ranking official in a noble household.
p.8, l.9: Belesgar – a literary nickname used in courtly love.
p.8, l.14: arch – Roman archway at Orange ('Aurenga'), nr. Avignon.

Marcabru's early career was spent as a jongleur working under the name of Panperdut. He was widely performed and admired for his political and satirical lines.

p.10, ll.16–18: After berating people for their laziness and carnality, an angry audience might throw their hats at the poet. He claims to be a scapegoat, because he cannot possibly know anything about the people.
'At the Fountain' shows the result of 12thc. crusading frenzy. King Louis has called the available men to serve him, and true lovers are parted.

Peire Cardenal's long life resulted in a huge output, and there is an online database dedicated to his work. Esteve de Belmont was a rival cleric.

p.15, ll.23–25: 'By this...' by the poem. These lines also carry the implication that Esteve poisoned his predecessor and an illegitimate child.

Rigaut de Berbezilh uses images from the medieval bestiary in several of his poems. He had trained as a knight, although he tends to depict himself as a retiring character.

p.16, l.7: court of Puy: Le Puy-en-Velay.
p.12, l.26: Berbezilh uses Dedalus for his image instead of Icarus.

Na Castelloza's work shows how the trobairitz was using the same strategies as her male counterpart, and expecting a return on her investment. There are four poems attributed to her.

p.21, ll.10–17: The poet is in a complex relationship where a fin amor suitor has been approved by her husband and family. Despite the aggravation he causes, she is willing to accept him back; she sends a barbed verse in the hope that he will recognise himself.
p.23, ll.1–3: When a knight pursues many partners, it brings shame on the knights. Na Castelloza proves her worth by being a skilful pleader for only one knight.

Bernart de Ventadorn was a classic trobar, specialising in love songs and the sensitive dilemmas of fin amor. There are translations by W.D. Snodgrass which preserve the rhyme schemes. One poem, 'Quan vei lausata mover' ('When I see the lark rising') is often recorded.

Giraut de Bornelh's lament ('planh') is for fellow trobar Raimbaut d'Aurenga, who died in May 1173 aged 29. The 'reis glorios' is one of the best-known dawn songs. Bornelh was regarded as a supreme master, performing at the courts of Richard 1 and Eleanor of Aquitaine.

p.26, l.14: 'Linhaure' is Bornelh's name for Raimbaut.
p.26, l.27: Poems were learnt by ear so an accurate and retentive memory was needed.
p.27, l.13: Velay – most likely Le Puy-en-Velay.
p.27, l.16: mystery – the craft of writing.
p.27, l.26: Proensa – Provence region. D'Aurenga was allied to the Berenger dynasty.

Peirol was a writer of conventional 'trobar leu' (light style) but some works see him engage with contemporary events.

p.31, ll.4–12: Love is referring to a crusade in the Holy Land – Peirol is unaware of the suffering and he ought to face reality, instead of giving advice about frivolous matters. He can observe a happy homecoming only if the 'Saladins' (Saracens) allow.

Comtessa de Dia may be a stage name, as are several others; she performed to a flute accompaniment, and the song given here is often recorded. There are four poems attributed to her, and the second example provides some idea of the confined, gossipy atmosphere in a noble house.

Guilhem de Peitieu (many variant spellings) was also William IX, Duke of Aquitaine. He can be traced through crusader literature as the leader of a disastrous campaign to recover the Holy Land in 1101.

p.35, l.18: St. Martial was a popular saint, with a centre of pilgrimage at Limoges.
p.35, ll.25–30: Guilhem satirises the poets' routine of seeking/pursuing a noble lady. But he is nevertheless secure, since his enemies (Normandy and France were separate states) are nowhere near her.
p.36, ll.11–12: His nonsense song concludes with an image of the written piece being locked in its recipient's personal valuables box, never to be seen again.

Arnaut Daniel was a writer of 'trobar clus' (ornate and difficult style, later known as 'trobar ric'). He was regarded as a master, originating several verse-forms.

p.37, ll:14–27: The poet outlines the process of becoming an accepted partner in fin amor. After successful petitioning, realisation dawns in the potential lover; and Arnaut is even more elaborate in his address. Meanwhile, embittered rival suitors are discarded.

Gaucelm Faidit was noted for his straightforward style. His dislike of sea travel resulted from a journey to the Holy Land.

Garsenda held the region of Montpellier and belonged to one of the country's most powerful dynasties. Her verse appears in a tenso with an unnamed correspondent.

Jofre Rudel's vida (brief biography, often apocryphal) outlines how he fell in love with the Countess of Tripoli, and died of a fever while undertaking a pilgrimage similar to the one he describes in the poem. He has been identified as a lord of Blaye (nr. Bordeaux) who took part in the Second Crusade, 1147.

FURTHER READING

There are online resources such as trobar.org, which contain most of the (male) repertoire and various translations.

Grammaires Provencales, ed. F. Guessard (Paris, 1858) is available online. This is based on a 13th century treatise and provides guidance on the language.

Articles about individual poets can be found online and on JSTOR, for example:

'Pois dompna s'ave/D'amar': Na Castellosa's Cansos and Medieval Feminist Scholarship, Alison Langdon (University of Oregon, 2001).

Selected Printed Books:

Lark in the Morning, ed. Robert Kehew (Chicago, 2005) A standard anthology, including translations by W.D. Snodgrass and Ezra Pound.

The Women Troubadours, Meg Bogin (W.W. Norton, 1980). Includes an introduction to life and culture in medieval Occitania.

113 Galician-Portuguese Troubadour Poems, ed. Richard Zenith (Carcanet, 1995). An anthology showing the parallel traditions across the Pyrenees.